W. H. Goss models. (Top row) Thistle vas[e ...]; Glastonbury Salt Cellar, 78 mm, Blackgan[g ... ...]nay, 118 mm, Mattock Bath. (Middle row) Bournemouth Bronze Urn, 50 mm, Tunbridge Wells; Winchester Pot, 75 mm, Margate; Gravesend Oriental Water Cooler, 76 mm, York. (Bottom row), Fenny Stratford Popper, 57 mm, Gloucester; Stirling Pint Measure, 60 mm, Folkestone; Waterlooville Soldier's Bottle, 85 mm, Sevenoaks; Las Palmas Ancient Jarra, 60 mm, Whitehaven.

GOSS AND OTHER CRESTED CHINA

Nicholas J. Pine

Shire Publica[tions]

CONTENTS

Copyright © 1984 by Nicholas J. Pine. First published 1984, reprinted 1986. Shire Album 120. ISBN 0 85263 662 8.

Set in 9 point Times and printed in Great Britain by C. I. Thomas & Sons (Haverfordwest) Ltd, Press Buildings, Merlins Bridge, Haverfordwest, Dyfed SA61 1XE.

COVER: *A W. H. Goss model, inscribed 'Model', of a costrel or farm labourer's water bottle of about the sixteenth century, made of local clay at St Mary's Pottery, Skimpot, and dug up on the site of the London and County Bank, Luton, May 1898. Registered number 630308. 65 mm, arms of Lynmouth.*

BELOW: *A W. H. Goss teaset comprising milk jug, 82 mm, cup and saucer, 70 mm, sugar basin, 48 mm and taper teapot and lid, 120 mm, decorated with green branches of red and yellow tomatoes.*

Attractive pieces of Goss. (Top) Cirencester Roman Urn (Hastings crest concealed), 165 mm, Hastings/St Leonards/Battle Abbey; (bottom row, left to right) unglazed bust of 'Beaconsfield' with the title impressed on the front of the plinth, 154 mm; diamond-mouthed vase, colour view of the 'Hereford Red Coat Man' 82 mm; unglazed bust of 'Gladstone', 167 mm.

INTRODUCTION

In the early 1960s it was becoming fashionable to collect Victoriana and in particular old china. Previously unsaleable, ivory coloured miniature artefacts bearing colourful coats of arms gradually began selling for sixpence a piece in junk shops. Most antique dealers, who previously would not have had such wares in their shop, began to stock the odd piece.

From a small band of collectors who began to make contact with one another in order to sell and swap to broaden their collections, the number of 'crestologists' collecting today has increased to several thousand, and the hobby is one of the fastest growing in the collecting field.

Heraldic souvenir china is the nearest three-dimensional collectable subject to stamps and postcards — but not so easy to find!

Pieces selling for sixpence and a shilling in the early 1960s, probably less than they were originally sold for between 1870 and 1930, when they were manufactured, were selling in 1984 for more than £3.00. A few particularly rare Goss cottages and memorials were even sold for more than a thousand pounds during the early 1980s. With ever more collectors joining the hunt for these exquisite treasures, prices of the better specimens will continue to rise.

Goss. (Top row) Large Norwich Urn, 92 mm, Dartmouth; 'Lady Rose', wearing crimson and blue crinoline, mauve overskirts and matching bonnet, carrying yellow basket of flowers, 170 mm, Goss England; Cenotaph, Whitehall, with green laurels at the side, 147 mm, Goss England, City of London. (Middle row) Thistle Vase, 78 mm, Luton; Old Swiss Milk Pot and lid, 86 mm, Lowestoft; Lincoln Vase, 65 mm, Horsham; Welsh Lady Candle Snuffer, white glazed, 100 mm; Herne Bay Brickfield Ewer, 88 mm, Totnes. (Bottom row) Kendal Jug, 88 mm, Wrexham; Bettws-y-Coed Ancient Bronze Kettle, Tunbridge Wells; egg-shaped salt cellar, Goss England with late colour transfer of river viaduct and church tower, 55 mm, Knaresborough; Bristol Puzzle Cider Cup, 50 mm, City of Durham/See of Durham/Durham University/University College, Durham.

4

A fine example of a W. H. Goss Winchester Castle Warden's Horn decorated with six lions rampant and transfers of William of Wykeham. The lettering around the plinth is in blue gothic script.

HERALDIC CHINA:
WHY IT WAS MADE AND WHEN

Although William Henry Goss of Stoke-on-Trent first produced some porcelain ornaments bearing the heraldic devices of notable public schools and colleges in Britain in the 1870s, it was not until the 1880s that his eldest son, Adolphus, began to market the idea nationally. He organised one agent in each town, seaside resort and city to sell the coat of arms of that place. He therefore had assured outlets for his souvenir wares, which consisted of several hundred different models of original artefacts, mainly copied from those found in museums, with an even wider range of coats of arms, transfer scenes and colourful decorations. During manufacture the black outline of the coat of arms was transfer-printed on to the china and then hand-coloured by an army of paintresses.

Collecting Goss china became an instant success mainly because the industrial boom in the cities and towns was spreading to the seaside resorts and countryside, where the working classes were now joining the middle classes on holiday. The development of the railway network across Britain and trips around the coast by paddle steamer allowed the previously home-bound workers the freedom of travel. As each resort became linked by train to the cities, so its tourist industry began to flourish.

It was important for the Victorian or Edwardian tourist to bring back a holiday memento. To go to Bournemouth, for example, and bring back a vase carrying the Bournemouth arms or, for those who could afford something more expensive, perhaps a china model of a pine cone, would be proof of the visit. The fun of collecting crested china lay in being able to obtain a certain crest in that particular place only, and nowhere else. If one wanted a Land's End crest, it could only be purchased at Land's End. The *Pottery Gazette* reviewed Goss heraldic porcelain in 1912. The favourable review stated: 'Goss has been something like a national benefactor in providing a number of

5

A fine selection of Goss. (Top row) Blackgang Tower, 118 mm, Worthing; teaplate, 'Golden Dog Quebec 1786', transfer on brown brickwork, 150 mm diameter, Quebec; Antwerp Oolen Pot, 'Trusty Servant' in colour, Antwerp, 72 mm. (Middle row) Seaford Roman Urn, 53 mm, Annan; Bath Roman Cup, 108 mm, Shrewsbury School; Stratford-upon-Avon Church Font, 50 mm, Shakespeare's arms. (Bottom row) Portland Vase, 53 mm, Greece; Winchester Black-jack, 46 mm, Warminster; one-handled mug with Adolphus Goss verse beginning, 'Goe not half way to meete a coming sorrowe', 37 mm; curve sided lip-salve pot and lid, 35 mm, Marlborough; straight-sided lip-salve pot and lid, 35 mm.

acceptable, artistic, and not too expensive presents for all occasions.'

Goss is the originator and best known manufacturer of heraldic china although many people mistakenly call all crested china 'Goss'. When the Goss factory started this collecting craze, other pottery manufacturers, mainly from the long established pottery district of Stoke-on-Trent, began rapidly to produce imitations. At first they tried to copy the ancient artefacts of Goss, but none could compete with the quality, because the factory's recipes and secrets were the results of years of experiments by W. H. Goss, who was also an eminent chemist. Instead, the other factories which exploited this craze for souvenirs chose to produce more light-hearted and cheaper shapes and these began to sell even more

6

readily, the manufacturers producing as much as would sell, with as many outlets in each area as could be obtained.

The Goss factory, however, refused to lower its standards, selling artistic shapes and allowing only perfect pieces to leave its premises. No pieces were knowingly sold with firing flaws, as this family firm valued its reputation more highly than its profits.

Goss china is easily distinguished from other makes. Its sober, classical style was much more suited to the middle class Victorian, and the quality of the parian body (a secret invention of W. H. Goss) was never captured nor equalled by any of the firm's rivals such as Arcadian, Carlton, Willow Art and Shelley. One does not have to be an expert to identify crested china. Almost every piece has a coat of arms on the front and a factory mark underneath on the base.

The Goss mark consists of either the black printed figure of an eagle with

Unusual Goss shapes. (Top row) Bust of Wordsworth, 164 mm; St Martin's Church Font, Canterbury, lidded and white glazed, 75 mm; early plate, glazed centre, moulded like a 'Toft' dish, 200 mm diameter. (Bottom row) Spanish Bull, 135 mm, Gibraltar; 'The Bridegroom, God help him', fully coloured, modelled after original designs by C. H. Twelvetrees; the Old Horseshoe with legend, 120 mm, Royal Field Artillery.

raised wings (a Gosshawk) with the printed *W. H. GOSS* underneath, or an impressed *W. H. GOSS* on the base, usually found on earlier pieces. A selection of the most popular marks used is shown below. The manufacturers' marks of the other major producers and of the more prolific firms are given on page 20. The history of these potteries and a sketch of each factory mark will be found in *Crested China* by Sandy Andrews. These number several hundred in all, but the firms mentioned here were the main rivals of Goss.

Gosshawk (showing registration mark).

The craze for collecting was at its height from the 1890s until the 1920s. Changing fashions and tastes led to its decline and during the First World War trade was poor. The depression of the 1930s turned public attention from collecting to the more serious problems of food and clothing and making ends meet.

W. H. Goss factory marks.
LEFT, TOP TO BOTTOM: *Serif impressed mark, c 1858-87; sans serif impressed mark, c 1887-1916; serif impressed mark, c 1887-1918 (showing registration date); longhand in W. H. Goss's own hand.*
BELOW: *Late Cottage Pottery, Goss England mark.*
BOTTOM: *Late Goss England mark.*

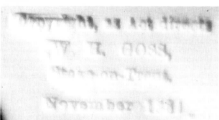

W H.GOSS
MADE IN ENGLAND

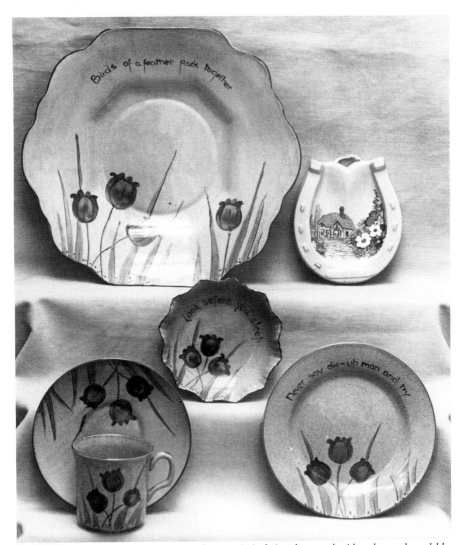

Goss England Cottage Pottery. The matching set is in beige decorated with red, purple and blue tulips and leaves and comprises a large shaped cake plate inscribed 'Birds of a feather flock together', 260 mm diameter; cup and saucer inscribed 'Tak a cup o'kindness' on reverse, 65 mm; nut tray inscribed, 'Look before you sleep', 118 mm diameter; teaplate inscribed 'Never say die — up man and try', 157 mm diameter. The Old Horseshoe has a hand-painted cottage garden scene.

The war had taken the firms' male employees to the front along with many of its customers, and after the war many who survived did not return to their former interests. Those crested china firms with little or no capital behind them could not survive the lack of business and either changed their products to such items as tiles or sanitary ware, went bankrupt or were taken over by other firms. The last piece of W. H. Goss china was made in 1929.

9

Goss. (Top row) Large plate, 200 mm diameter, with arms of the City of Lincoln surrounded by flags of the First World War allies, Great Britain, France, Russia, Japan, Servia, Belgium and Italy; Southport Vase, 50 mm, with Welsh emblems of mistletoe and a golden sickle, and crossed daggers on the rear; large wall pocket, 173 mm, Warwick/Earl of Leicester/Bear and Ragged Staff (R L stands for Robert Leicester). (Middle row, left) Old Gateway on Monnow Bridge, Monmouth, 103 mm, Deal; (right) Goss England Royal Buff dish with two handles and colour transfer of Exeter Cathedral. (Bottom row) Art Deco style vase, two handles, with green, yellow and blue geometric pattern; thistle-shaped vase with two handles, 75 mm, Gloucester; St Martin's Cross, Iona, brown, unglazed to simulate stone and tinged with green moss; Wordsworth's birthplace, Cockermouth, pale yellow walls with blue windows and dark green ivy climbing the walls.

Rare W. H. Goss coloured Powder Bowl with decorated lid, 100 mm diameter. The floral spray in the centre of the lid has a yellow rose, orange forget-me-nots and green leaves in relief. The base has ribbed sides striped in a delicate shade of yellow.

A BRIEF HISTORY OF THE FIRM OF W. H. GOSS

As William Henry Goss was the inventor of heraldic porcelain, it is his name that is the best known in connection with this ware. He was born in London in 1833 and studied at the school of design at Somerset House. While he was in London he joined artistic and literary circles and made many important friendships and contacts which were later to help him in his career. One such friend was Alderman W. F. M. Copeland, then Lord Mayor of London and owner of the Copeland Spode works in Stoke-on-Trent, and it was under his guidance that William Goss studied chemistry and pottery. He later worked for Copeland as a designer at the Spode works in Stoke-on-Trent. He was soon promoted to chief designer and modeller. The following year, when he was only twenty-five years old, he left Copeland and set up his own small firm nearby, concentrating on a small production of exquisite high class ornamental parian ware, figures and terracotta.

In 1872 he perfected and patented several improvements to the manufacture of jewelled porcelain and this, together with the success of the recently introduced parian busts, seems to have prompted a move to larger premises. The address of this new factory was London Road, Stoke. By 1883 Adolphus, Williams's eldest son, had joined the management of the firm. There was less demand for the expensive hand-thrown ornaments, and a growing market, as Adolphus could see, for cheaper, less ornate ware. He realised that with the recent improvements in education and transport there was a market for mass-produced souvenirs for the day trippers who were now visiting places that had previously been inaccessible to them. With this in mind he developed an idea of his father's, who had for some time been decorating small pots and vases with the coats of arms of public schools, hospitals and especially the Oxford and Cambridge colleges at the request of Goss's trade

Medium range Goss cottages. (Top row, left) Cat and Fiddle Inn at Buxton, the highest inn in England, 65 mm long; (right) Manx Cottage, large nightlight version, 122 mm long. (Middle row) The Old Thatched Cottage at Poole, 68 mm long; A Window in Thrums, 60 mm long; Old Maids Cottage at Lee, Devon, 75 mm long. (Bottom row, left) St Nicholas Chapel, Ilfracombe, 74 mm long; (right) Lloyd George's Early Home with Annexe, 100 mm long.

Attractively decorated Goss. (Top row, left) Large Norwich Urn, 86 mm, Royal Standard of England; (right) sugar basin and milk jug, edged in blue with hand-painted pink, blue and maroon crocuses. (Bottom row) Ball Vase with crinkle top and early moth decoration in gold and red, 67 mm; large Japan Ewer, trimmed with black and covered in large bright orange, blue, purple and yellow poppies, 200 mm; Parian Globe Inkwell, glazed inside well, three sprays of green and purple thistles, 70 mm; Ball Vase, crinkle top, two extinct butterflies in shades of red and brown, 52 mm.

customers in these towns.

Adolphus first introduced a few basic historical models from different parts of Britain, such as the Gloucester Jug and the Itford Lewes Urn. Upon these he placed either the corresponding coat of arms, for example a Gloucester Jug would carry either the arms of the town of Gloucester or the see of Gloucester, or a colourful decoration such as transfers of seagulls or floral sprays. Another early design was that of butterflies, all painted accurately in the Goss tradition in the correct colours and proportions. Many of these butterflies, common then, are now extinct.

The success of the venture was so great that the range of historical models (all clearly named on the side or base) was extended and the coats of arms, or crests as they were popularly but incorrectly called, were increased. Eventually, any model could be ordered with any crest through the right agents. Adolphus organised the expansion and was the firm's chief travelling salesman, establishing agencies in almost every town throughout Britain, and also gaining permission from each council and parish to reproduce its coat of arms on his china. He also took photographs for reproducing as scenic transfers on china and made sketches of all kinds of ancient pottery shapes and vessels from museums and collections from which the firm could make miniatures. Adolphus became an expert photographer and even developed his own negatives. He was away on his travels so much during the 1880s and 1890s that his wife and family rarely saw him. By the time of his father's death in 1906 he had established over one thousand agencies in Great Britain.

One of his best ideas was to produce coloured models of famous buildings such as Shakespeare's house at Stratford-upon-Avon. He began these in 1893 and they became a very popular range. They did not bear coats of arms, nor did the series of brown crosses and some other unglazed monuments. All the coloured examples of Goss are perfectly modelled and faithfully hand-painted to reproduce exactly the originals from which they were copied.

By 1902 two of William's other sons had joined Adolphus in management and they decided to treble the size of their factory to cope with the enormous number of orders which were arriving from Britain and other countries, for Adolphus had travelled in several continents and gained worldwide custom.

After 1913 the firm's fortunes were not good. Huntley Goss, who was now in sole charge, was as traditional as his late father and failed to move with the times,

even refusing to have a telephone installed. During the war most of the overseas agencies never paid for the goods shipped out under the normal three months credit terms.

A few 'war' models were made at the outbreak of hostilities in 1914, including models of some shells and a tank. But these merely duplicated the activities of the factory's competitors, who had already established a dominant share in the market for military china. A temporary respite was gained when Goss produced a range of regimental and battleship crests together with the crests

Goss. (Top row) Giant bulbous vase with cup top and strap handle, 180 mm, Aylesbury, Buckinghamshire; butter dish with ears of corn and 'Waste Not' in relief, 143 mm diameter, Finsbury; Melrose Cup, 130 mm, Hastings. (Bottom row) Bath Bronze Roman Ewer, 120 mm, Knaresborough Abbey; large Bag-ware Sack Vase in apricot lustre, 130 mm; Blackpool Tower, 120 mm, Dunster.

Larger Goss models. (Top row) Large Cambridge Jug, 94 mm, Cambridge; large Southwold Ancient Jar, 142 mm, Southwold; Welsh Jack and lid, 118 mm, colour transfer of Caernarvon Castle/Caernarvon, arms of HRH The Prince of Wales. (Middle row) Steyning Sea Urchin, 50 mm, Manor of Bramber; Burton Beer Barrel, 60 mm, Burton upon Trent; large Dart Sack Bottle, 94 mm, Dartmouth; Bournemouth Pilgrim Bottle, 88 mm, Bournemouth. (Bottom row) Winchester Pot, 74 mm, City of Winchester, Hampshire; Bournemouth Ancient Egyptian Lamp, Bournemouth; the Nose of Brasenose, Oxford college, Brasenose College.

Goss First World War military decorations and badges. (Top row) Folkestone Roman Ewer, 95 mm, four flags of the Allies; Bag-ware plate, with an amusing but gruesome verse 'To Cook a German', surrounded by flags of the Allies, 152 mm diameter; crinkle-top conical vase, 70 mm, seven flags of the Allies. (Bottom row) Carlisle Salt Pot, 42 mm, Durham Light Infantry; Glastonbury Ancient Vase, 46 mm, Notts and Derby; Exeter Vase, 62 mm, Inns of Court OTC; Exeter Vase, 61 mm, Royal Flying Corps; Swindon Vase, 55 mm, Army Ordnance Corps; Silchester Reading Roman Urn, 55 mm, London Scottish.

of the French towns where the troops were stationed. It is to Huntley's credit that the standard of porcelain used in the manufacture of these military items was kept up and that so much care was taken over the hand painting of the crests and the gilding. Even today most Goss militaria looks as if it were newly made.

Various attempts were made in the 1920s to revive the firm's fortunes but, when close to bankruptcy at the end of the decade, the family sold out to a competitor, Harold Taylor Robinson, who owned Arcadian China. Until 1940 most of the china produced at the Goss factory was marked *Goss England*. Production of crested china ceased altogether around 1940.

RIGHT: *Some of the largest and the smallest Goss wares. (Top row) Gigantic vase with two handles, 200 mm, Devon; Portland Vase, 51 mm, Weymouth; Globe Vase with three small knurled handles and narrow neck, 196 mm, St Leonards/Battle Abbey/Hastings. (Second row) Beaker, 80 mm, Newport, Isle of Wight; Eton Vase, 86 mm, Ruthin; Egyptian Water Jar, 56 mm, Fulham; Pompeian Ewer, 91 mm, Burgh of Rothesay; Egyptian Mocca Cup (bowl shaped), 40 mm, Eastbourne. (Third row) Late teaplate, 175 mm diameter, Stowmarket; Cylinder Vase on three feet, 35 mm, Tavistock; Melon Cream Jug, 53 mm, Pevensey; Cone Vase, 56 mm, Aylesbury. (Bottom row) Nottingham Ewer, 63 mm, Folkestone; Exeter Vase, 63 mm, Clacton on Sea; Newbury Leather Bottle, 58 mm, Stratford-upon-Avon; Irish Bronze Pot, 43 mm, Bognor; Cambridge Pitcher, 63 mm, City of Salisbury.*

17

THE PRODUCTS OF THE GOSS FACTORY

The shapes modelled from original ancient ewers and vessels in museums and other places around Britain are known as *named models* because the factory printed a description, usually on the base, or, if the bottom was too small, on the rear of the piece. This makes it very easy to identify each model and even a novice collector can appear knowledgeable when showing a collection to friends. The named models number over six hundred and can be found bearing almost any of the seven thousand coats of arms and decorations. The artefacts are representative of each area in Great Britain as well as of some other countries. Most towns and cities had their own shape as well as coats of arms. Blackpool, for example, was represented by Blackpool Tower, which is a white glazed building and a good attempt at a reproduction of the original tower, which is still standing. Some of the buildings and memorial stones and crosses copied by Goss are no longer in existence. The Old Thatched Cottage, Poole, is a fairly scarce, coloured Goss cottage, modelled in the nineteenth century from the original building in the old town of Poole, which no longer still stands. Such was the exactness of the Goss factory that the Goss reproduction shows us precisely how the cottage used to look.

Some towns are represented by a vase, such as Southport by the Southport Vase, with the inscription on the base *Model of Vase found in Southport during excavations.* Ludlow was represented by the Ludlow Sack Bottle, and Maidstone by the Maidstone Roman Ewer. Maldon in Essex had the Maldon Incendiary Bomb, whereas some places were allocated several models, such as Malta with the Maltese Carafe, Double-mouthed Vase, Fire Grate, Funereal Urn, Twin Vase, Two-wick Lamp and Maltese Vase à Canard. Adolphus Goss's trip to Malta had to be made worthwhile and shipments of orders large enough to be profitable had to be made.

Whilst vases, ewers and urns make up the bulk of the range of models, there is an exciting mixture of bottles, bowls, buckets, stones, lobster traps, fossils, castles, skulls and pipkins, even a Canadian Maple Leaf. If one visits the place of origin of a Goss model, one can usually still find the original, especially if it was an ancient Roman or Saxon piece of pottery in a museum. For example, anyone looking at the Ballafletcher Cup in Douglas Museum, Isle of Man, would be surprised and pleased to see how accurately it had been copied by Goss. The original, however, was made of glass and was transparent.

The Egyptian pieces (made about 1913) must have provoked great excitement amongst Goss collectors of the day, because fifteen different models were produced, including the Great Pyramid of Gizeh. Egyptian crests included the Egyptian flag as well as the country's coat of arms and the city of Cairo, and they are very colourful.

There is a series of certain shapes which fortunately fall into easy collecting categories. These include lighthouses, shoes, league models, lamps, cups, fonts, crosses and animals. The league models were made especially for members of the League of Goss Collectors, formed in 1900: each member received a 'Portland Vase', bearing the league arms, free on joining, and one different new model every year on payment of the subscription. In 1918 the league became the International League of Goss Collectors, with a more colourful device to decorate the annual league models. These were continued until 1932 and the last six are particularly scarce because membership declined rapidly in the last few years.

An enterprising young man called J. J. Jarvis conceived the idea of the League and he began *The Goss Record*, a booklet published at irregular intervals, listing the latest range of Goss models and prices and a full list of stockists. The first edition appeared in 1900 and the ninth and last in 1921. It was a necessary publication for enthusiasts who needed the information it contained in order to plan trips for adding to their collection. The Gosses, surprisingly, disliked Jarvis's businesslike approach and he had difficulty in continually getting the information on the products and agents, but undoubtedly his

Goss domestic wares. (Top row) Large Melon milk jug, 118 mm, Portsmouth; tiny one-handled mug, with illuminated verse by Adolphus Goss beginning 'Goe not halfe way to meete', 36 mm; butter dish in wooden surround, 155 mm diameter, Bournemouth. (Middle row, left) Melon cream jug, 53 mm, City of Exeter; (right) ball-shaped sugar basin, 55 mm, Ripon. (Bottom row) Cup, saucer and plate, decorated with flocks of blue and grey seagulls, 175 mm diameter; egg-shaped pepper pot, 60 mm, Bexhill; cylinder egg cup, 60 mm, Kingston-upon-Thames; taper cup and saucer, covered in green shamrocks, 60 mm.

work helped trade.

Any Goss model bearing the crest of any town has a certain basic value for the piece alone, but if the arms are the correct matching ones for that piece then a premium should be added. In *The Price Guide to Goss China* a Salisbury Leather Gill with any crest was listed in 1986 at £10.00, but with any of the Salisbury arms it would be valued at £24.50.

There were also variations in sizes. Many of the models were made in both large and small sizes, and a few even had a middle size. There may be slight differences in similar pieces of the same 'size' but this is due to the 10 per cent shrinkage experienced during firing. Not all pieces shrank at exactly the same rate, so if you have a model which is 5 mm smaller than the size recorded in *The*

Price Guide to Goss China then you will not have found an unrecorded size!

The Goss cottages were made in a range of sizes from 1893, with some being produced also in the form of nightlights. Cottages were made glazed or unglazed, the latter being slightly more usual, but this does not affect the values. Each piece should bear a paintress's mark on the base, in whichever colour she was last using on the piece. Each had her own mark, and if a piece was considered faulty when it was checked then the paintress could be traced and duly chastened. A paintress responsible for too many badly coloured pieces would be dismissed, so high standards of work were maintained.

Two of the cottages appear with roofs of two distinctly different colours; these are the Goss Oven and First and Last House. The cheapest Goss cottages (apart from damaged ones) are Ann Hathaway's and Shakespeare's, after the originals in Stratford-upon-Avon. The most popular selling cottages at the time were the prettiest, most attractive and most accessible, and the cottages which are considered scarce today are usually the less glamorous, perhaps plainer and based on originals situated in remoter areas. In Edwardian times Stratford was a very popular tourist resort, so the two Goss Stratford cottages sold very well.

The range of fonts and crosses includes many without coats of arms. Such religious models look better without crests, especially unglazed, and they often look as if they are made of stone. Some crosses are tinted with brown, green or grey to give the appearance of moss tinging the stone. These can be valuable, ranging in 1986 from around £35 for the Richmond Market Cross to £875 for St Iltyd's Church Font at Llantwit Major in Wales.

The best value amongst Goss wares is the vast array of ornamental and domestic ware. *The Price Guide to Goss China* shows a photograph of almost every shape and names each piece, with suitable references to *The Goss Records* where possible. As well as tea sets and table requisites, even a complete dinner service has been recorded. There are several styles of tea service, but the prettiest is the Bag-ware, in which each piece is made to look like a bag, with a gathered rim tied with a blue ribbon. With cups and saucers, the cup is tied at the rim, and a blue cordlike handle attached, the saucer being gathered underneath. A cup and saucer bearing different crests are worth only half the price of a correctly matched pair.

Goss decorations were most prolific in the domestic wares. *Goss China, Arms, Decorations and Their Values* by Nicholas J. Pine lists every known Goss decoration — some seven thousand in all. The types of crest include towns and cities, foreign, educational, ecclesiastical, organisations, royal and commemorative, monochrome and polychrome transfer-printed pictorial views, regimental and naval, armours, flags, masonic and flora and fauna. Many decorations add a substantial premium to the value of a model.

Crested china factory marks. (*Top row*) Arcadian China, Carlton Ware, Grafton China. (*Bottom row*) Shelley China, Swan China, Willow Art China.

A crested alcohol collection. *(Top row) Drunkard with tankard, 'It's better to be alive with 18d than dead with a thousand pounds', 75 mm, Exeter, Willow Art; 'Mr Pussyfoot, all water, we don't think!' (standing next to a water pump), 100 mm, Deal, Podmore; bottle with cork, 'One special Scotch', 98 mm, Cardinal Wolsey, Arcadian; beer lover draining beer barrel, 'Beer hic beer — glorious hic beer', 79 mm, Newmarket, Carlton. (Bottom row) Beer barrel on stand, 58 mm, Paddington, Arcadian; upright beer barrel, 64 mm, Clacton, Foley No 48; chair, 'Tak hold an sup lad', 79 mm, Yorkshireman's Arms, Tuscan; champagne bottle pepper pot, 100 mm, Bournemouth, Grafton; beer bottle, 91 mm, Sandringham, Carlton; hand holding beer glass, 48 mm, Clacton-on-Sea, Willow Art.*

THE PRODUCTS OF OTHER MANUFACTURERS

Most of the potteries producing similar crested china concentrated their efforts upon the main themes of military subjects, buildings, animals and transport. In her book *Crested China*, Sandy Andrews studies the output of all these factories and categorises the products under the following headings: busts, ancient artefacts, coloured buildings, white glazed buildings, monuments and crosses, historical/folklore, traditional and national souvenirs, seaside souvenirs, countryside, animals, birds, Great War, memorabilia, memorials, home/nostalgic, comic/novelty, cartoon/comedy characters, alcohol, sport, musical instruments, transport, 'modern' equipment, hats and shoes, and miniature domestic.

Busts were modelled of many famous people of the period, including leading politicians, royalty and other public figures. The First World War influenced the potteries to make busts of the war leaders including Lord Jellicoe, General Joffre, Lord Kitchener and Lord Roberts. The bases of the busts vary in shape and size from round to square, plain or shaped plinths, with or without coats of arms. Busts of royalty, subjects usually including the then reigning King and Queen and the Prince and Princess of Wales, are much sought after.

Coloured buildings or cottages are not normally found crested. Willow Art made the largest range, and probably the best. The Hewitt Brothers, the owners, were rightly proud of their products. Particularly pretty examples are the Dick Whittington Inn near Stourbridge, the Old Maids Cottage at Lee, near Ilfracombe, and the Bell Hotel, Abel Fletcher's House. The cottages are usually 2½ inches (64 mm) long in the small sizes and 6-7 inches (150-175 mm) long in the larger, with certain models made to a bigger scale.

White glazed buildings are very impressive, especially when displayed in groups. This area includes bridges, hop kilns, cathedrals (both the whole building and the fronts only, with flat backs), churches, clock towers and castles. Always check the pinnacles of the churches, as these are prone to damage. Chesterfield Parish Church AD 1307 is true to the original with the twisted spire, so if you find one do not reject it because the spire looks bent!

Crested buildings. (Top row) 'First and Last House in England' with green door, 84 mm, Penzance, Willow Art' 'Lincoln Cathedral West Front', 105 mm, City of Lincoln, Podmore; 'God's Providence House AD 1652', 90 mm, Chester, Podmore. (Middle row) Brick cottage with thatched roof, 55 mm, colour transfer of 'West Promenade and Pavilion, Rhyl', British manufacture; St Paul's Cathedral, 90 mm, City of London, Alexandra; 'First and Last Refreshment House in England' (note the table and chairs outside), 68 mm, Falmouth, Grafton. (Bottom row) 'Model of Old Chapel on Lantern Hill, Ilfracombe, Devon', 50 mm; Guildhall, Portsmouth, 58 mm, City of Portsmouth, Arcadian; miniature Big Ben, 93 mm, City of London, Botolph; 'Model of Burns Cottage' (with historic inscription on the reverse), 70 mm long, Ayr, Savoy.

Crested monuments and castles. (Top row) 'The Monument, Laceby' (dedicated to a Norwegian couple and their four children), 140 mm; 'Highland Mary' statue, 155 mm, Glasgow, Regis; 'Lifeboat Memorial, Caister on Sea', 170 mm, Willow Art. (Middle row) 'Dover Patrol' War Memorial, 125 mm, Dover, Arcadian; Blackpool Tower, 125 mm, Horsham, British manufacture; 'Hall Cross', 155 mm, Impero; 'John Ruskin Memorial', 120 mm, Coniston, Carlton. (Bottom row) Hastings Castle Ruins, 88 mm, Hastings, Carlton; 'Baron Burton Memorial', 130 mm, Burton upon Trent, Clifton; Farnham Castle in pearl lustre, 97 mm, Farnham, Carlton.

Crested hats. (Top row) Parian straw boater with pale blue petersham band, 95 mm long; Welsh hat, blue band, 57 mm long, Worthing, Willow Art; straw boater 74 mm long, Sidmouth, Swan China; top hat, bear and ragged staff, 40 mm. (Second row) Extra large Welsh hat, 71 mm, Llandudno with full spelling of Llanfair P.G. round the brim, Saxony; crisp Luton boater with blue and white band; Welsh hat, 58 mm, Beaumaris, Victoria. (Third row) Welsh hat, 55 mm, Hednesford, Shelley No 154; trilby, 96 mm long, Chepstow, Shelley No 500; colonial hat, 91 mm diameter, Doncaster, Carlton. (Bottom row) Model of ancient coaching hat inscribed 'Oh where did you get that hat!', colour transfer of mother hen and chicks on green grass, 40 mm, Arcadian; John Bull style top hat, 40 mm, Shrewsbury, Grafton; top hat, 40 mm, Oxford University, Shelley; Welsh hat, ribbed band, 40 mm.

Crested footwear. (Top row, left to right) Kitten in boot, 65 mm, Frome, Pearl Arms; highboot, 64 mm, Great Yarmouth, Carlton; highboot, 100 mm, Bury St Edmunds, Arcadian; laced shoe, 80 mm; baby on bootee, 76 mm, Herne Bay, British manufacture. (Bottom row, left to right) Clog, 105 mm long, colour transfer of Hastings Castle, British manufacture; lady's shoe with heel, 90 mm long, Croydon, Gemma; ankle boot, 70 mm long, Llanelly, Carlton; lady's eighteenth-century shoe, 95 mm long, Tenby, Coronet Ware; Lancashire clog 90 mm long, City of Exeter, no factory mark.

Castle ruins are especially interesting, amongst the best being the Hastings Castle Ruins. Under the heading monuments and crosses, a variety of ancient stones can be included. A collection of these could include the more common Rufus Stone, a strange three-sided object with inscriptions on each side, like the original in the New Forest. Also in this theme are the Great Rock of Ages in Somerset; the Maiwand Memorial, which is a statue of a lion on a plinth, from the Forbury Gardens in Reading; the Statue of King Alfred in Winchester; crosses such as the Sandbach Crosses; and monuments which include Nelson's Column, Trafalgar Square, complete with lions at the base.

Pieces based on legends and historical events, such as models of the execution block, the ducking stool (this is made of two parts hinged together), coaching hats and archbishops' chairs, make up the section called historical and folklore. Characters such as Peeping Tom and Lady Godiva of Coventry, the Trusty Servant of Winchester and the English

Folksong Bride beside her chest are some of the figures depicted either as models or as transfers decorating various shapes. The Bride with the chest or trunk is believed to be the bride in folksongs who played hide and seek on her wedding night, hid in a chest and was never found. Her skeleton, however, was discovered many years later.

Traditional and national souvenirs include regional foods such as the Cornish pasty and Cheddar cheese (sometimes coloured like the real cheese), types of Lancashire clog, once a common sight amongst mill workers in the north, Luton boaters complete with coloured bands moulded in china which look like real petersham, and Scottish thistle vases, Welsh hats and Manx leg symbols. Ethnic souvenirs were produced in abundance by the potteries, particularly Irish, Welsh and Scottish pieces with their leeks, harps, jaunting cars and bagpipes.

The tourist industry in coastal resorts led to large numbers of seaside souvenirs being sold. Tiny china crabs, a variety of shells, yachts and paddle steamers, busts

Crested cats. (Top row) Cat playing with lute, 54 mm, Margate, Saxony; cat singing, reading sheet music, 68 mm, Ryde, Saxony; giant furry cat, with large ruff, 106 mm, Bath, Corona; miniature black cat in wooden chair, pearl lustre, 76 mm, Whitley Bay, Carlton; long-necked cat, 108 mm, Chippenham, Arcadian. (Bottom row) Large Cheshire cat, grinning, 100 mm, Littlehampton, Arcadian; kitten with blue bow, 59 mm, Sidmouth, Carlton; cat ready to pounce, 90 mm long, Worthing, Saxony; angry cat with arched back, raised tail, 82 mm, Wimborne, Arcadian.

of lifeboatmen, lighthouses complete with rocky bases, Punch and Judy shows, fish baskets with lids and bathing machines are all legacies of the seaside holiday of the past. How different the holiday scene must have looked then. Appealing to similar tastes would be the countryside shapes, such as acorns, leaves, haystacks, pine cones, tree trunks fashioned into vases or hatpin holders, and even a farmer with his plough.

One of the most important themes was crested animals. Queen Mary popularised these and while she was Princess of Wales she would have her collection packed up and taken with her on visits away from home and unpacked and displayed to make guest bedrooms seem more like home. The majority of animals produced were household pets and

RIGHT: *Crested buildings and monuments. (Top row) Thatched cottage, 48 mm, Willesden, Royal Arms China; 'The Castle, Guildford', full of detail including a dungeon, steps up to door, pierced windows and climbing ivy, 130 mm, Guildford; 'Burns Statue', 177 mm, Ayr, Thistle China; Fisherman's Memorial, 127 mm, Southend-on-Sea, Saxony China. (Second row) Irish Round Tower with green shamrocks around base, 132 mm, Dublin, Carlton; Chester, God's Providence House, 81 mm, Chester, Arcadian; 'Interior of Burns' Cottage' with furniture in relief, 124 mm long; Tom Tower, Christchurch, Oxford, with arms on the reverse, 130 mm, Kidderminster, Carlton. (Third row) 'Round Tower, Windsor Castle', 68 mm, Windsor, Willow Art; 'Monnow Gate, Monmouth', 106 mm, arms of Monmouth, Savoy; 'The Smallest House in Great Britain', 92mm, Conway, Grafton; 'Model of Guildhall', 56 mm, Portsmouth, Arcadian. (Bottom row, left) Large bridge with grassy banks, 134 mm long, Faringdon, Corona; (right) 'Worcester Cathedral', 146 mm long, Worcester, Willow Art.*

farmyard animals. Swans were made in vast quantities, but ducks were not. Posy holders, including swans with open wings, were used in most households for displaying flowers in a delightful way. More exotic animals were much more expensive and therefore are very scarce now. Serious studies of animals usually fetch the highest prices although the comical and amusing animals can be very appealing. The coloured series of miniature Black Cats by Arcadian and Willow depict black cats in about thirty different poses, all of which are very collectable, especially the 'sporty' ones such as the black cat in a canoe, and riding a bicycle. The birds include ornate lustre peacocks with feathers outstretched, pelicans with amusing inscriptions relating to their full beaks, chicks hatching out of their eggs, chicken salt and pepper pots, wise owls with one eye shut or wearing mortar boards to indicate their wisdom, storks, seagulls and a novelty item called the Norwich Warbler with a mouthpiece in the tail for whistling or blowing bubbles.

The Great War is the most collected theme, most factories producing their own designs in their haste to get topical new models into the shops. The most sought-after mementoes are models of soldiers, sailors and nurses. The Russian Cossack on horseback is a good find, as is the British Cavalry Officer, also on horseback. Busts of sailors can be found with their ship's name impressed on their hatband whilst those of soldiers can have military verses, such as 'Hearts of Oak', printed on their backs, and the words *Tommy Atkins* or *Territorial,* for example, on their peaked caps. One horrific model is of a soldier wearing a respirator.

Aeroplanes are often fine specimens, some having a separate movable propeller. Biplanes can sometimes be found painted with red, white and blue roundels. Various types of airship and zeppelin serve as reminders of the way the war was fought, and bombs and shells were modelled just like the originals, but not to scale.

A collection of battleships and minesweepers can look superb, and even now a new ship occasionally comes to light as old collections are found. Vehicles such as tanks and armoured cars were produced as quickly as their photographs appeared in the national newspapers depicting the latest battle scenes, the war leaders having hitherto kept their weapons secret. Cheaper war products include drums, Gurkha knives, water bottles, helmets and boots.

An area which is always amusing is comic/novelty. Most of these delightful models were made in the late 1920s and are brightly coloured and good fun. Some can be compared to fairings, like the couple in bed inscribed *John, is everything shut up for the night? — All but you darling!* Married couples are targets for humour, as are nagging wives, suffragettes and policemen. The famous Gilbert and Sullivan line 'A policeman's lot is not a happy one' can occasionally be found inscribed on a fat, jolly, crested policeman. The billiken, a strange god-like creature which was invented in America in 1908 by Florence Pretz, was a happy little 'God of Luck' which had crossed the Atlantic and won the hearts of the English. It soon appeared in souvenir china form.

The cartoon characters and comedians of the 1920s are virtually unknown now — but we have crested china models to remind us of the nation's jokers at that time. Harry Lauder and his Tam o' Shanter, Ally Sloper, the first English comic strip character in the early years of the twentieth century, complete with shining red nose and drunken posture, Mrs Gummidge and her umbrella, together with odd little characters like Mr Pickwick, were known nationally in those days.

An unexpected theme, alcohol, has provided a wide range of beer barrels, silvered tankards and beer bottles on trays, champagne in ice buckets, drunken monks holding whisky glasses, soda siphons and corked beer bottles.

Sport was as important in the 1920s as it is now, and cricket bats, holdalls, tennis rackets, golf balls and footballs were featured prominently in heraldic ware, so the prices realised by these items are moderate.

There was a delicate assortment of musical instruments, from banjos, double basses and guitars to pianos, violins and tambourines. Violins are scarce, but not

Crested First World War models. (Top row) Bill Sykes's Dog, 'My word if you're not off', 60 mm, Bedlington, Arcadian; nurse standing, 'Soldier's friend', 135 mm, Warminster, Arcadian; munitions worker, 'Doing her bit', 104 mm, City of London, Carlton; model of observer sausage balloon, 80 mm, Tonbridge, Arcadian. (Middle row) British machine gun, 100 mm long, Wallasey, Carlton; sailor winding capstan, 110 mm, Hythe, Hants, Arcadian; biplane with fixed propeller, 120 mm long, City of Bristol, Arcadian. (Bottom row) Renault tank, 115 mm long, Lowestoft, Corona; 'Model of German Incendiary Bomb' with Victory of Justice inscription, 88 mm, Thorpe Bay, Carlton; 'HMS War Spite' battleship, 158 mm long, Redcar, Carlton.

so the various other instruments.

Transport is a very collectable area. The charabanc or single-decker bus was modelled with a variety of differences in number of seats, headlamps, windscreen sizes and lengths of running boards. Also classified under transport are the can of petrol which is impressed *Motor Spirit* and a petrol pump of the time. The range of vehicles made was large but, with the exception of charabancs, few were made in great numbers.

'Modern' equipment appertains to what was modern in the 1920s, not today. A gramophone in an upright cabinet was the latest in music, and so were the

29

varieties with horns. The crested cameras made were the folding variety, and the oven is an amazing model.

Hats and shoes cover a huge range of different styles. These include top hats, bishops' mitres, Boy Scouts' hats, Welsh hats and clogs, heeled ladies' shoes, babies' boots and even hobnail boots.

Miniature domestic items such as thimbles, cheese dishes and watering cans are amusing and were highly thought of in the Edwardian era, as were the enormous ranges of domestic ware. As so many hair tidies, candlesticks, trinket jars and the like exist now, they must have been very popular in the early 1900s.

Crested chairs. (Top row) Archbishop of Canterbury's Chair, 93 mm, City of Canterbury, Arcadian; model of James V's chair at Stirling Castle, 100 mm, Wolverhampton, Willow Art; 'The Old Arm Chair' with verse, 115 mm, Bournemouth, Carlton; Mr Beetle and Sunny Jim in armchair, 90 mm, Folkestone, Hewitt Bros. (Bottom row) Coronation Chair, 'Tak hod an sup lad', 78 mm, Tuscan; Souter Johnny on seat, bisque china, coloured figure with no crest, 110 mm, German; Billiken on throne, 'The God of things as they ought to be', 100 mm, Derby, Podmore; 'The Old Armchair', 90 mm, Ramsgate, Florentine; model of Mary Queen of Scots' Chair, Edinburgh Castle, 80 mm, Richmond, Willow.

LEFT: Crested First World War military models. (Top row) Bust of Albert, King of the Belgians, 156 mm, Whitley Bay, Savoy; cannon shell, 72 mm, Shoeburyness, Arcadian; bust of French, 'United we stand', four flags, 165 mm, no factory mark; bust of 'Kitchener' on glazed base, 120 mm, Aldershot, Savoy. (Middle row) Bust of sailor 'HMS Queen Elizabeth', 92 mm, Rosyth, Arcadian; British naval gun, 54 mm, Perth, Carlton; 'HRH Prince of Wales' statue, 154 mm, City of London, Podmore; British aerial bomb, 76 mm, Ruislip, Arcadian. (Bottom row) Armoured car, 126 mm long, Bournemouth, Diamond China; British trench mortar gun, 102 mm, Bournemouth, Diamond China; revolver, 84 mm long, Malmesbury Abbey, Arcadian.

FURTHER READING

Andrews, Sandy. *Crested China*. Milestone Publications, 1980.

Andrews, Sandy and Pine, Nicholas. *The Price Guide to Crested China*. Milestone Publications, 1984.

Emery, Norman. *William Henry Goss and Goss Heraldic China*. George Street Press City Museum, Stoke on Trent, 1971.

Galpin, John. *A Handbook of Goss China*. Milestone Publications, 1972.

Hedges, A. A. C. *Let's Collect Goss China*. Jarrolds, 1979.

Jarvis, J. J. *Goss Record War Edition*. Milestone Publications, 1979 (reprinted).

Magee, John D. *Goss for Collectors: The Literature*. Milestone Publications, 1984.

Pine, Nicholas. *The Price Guide to Goss China*. Milestone Publications, 1986.

Pine, Nicholas. *Goss China, Arms, Decorations and their Values*. Milestone Publications, 1982.

Southall, Robert. *Take Me Back to Dear Old Blighty*. Milestone Publications, 1981.

Ward, Roland. *The Price Guide to the Models of W. H. Goss*. Antique Collectors Club, 1981.

PLACES TO VISIT

Botanic Gardens Museum, Churchtown, Southport, Merseyside PR9 7NB. Telephone: Southport (0704) 27547.

Dawlish Museum, The Knowle, Barton Terrace, Dawlish, Devon.

Egham Museum, Literary Institute, High Street, Egham, Surrey TW20 9EW. Telephone: Egham (0784) 36645.

Epping Forest District Museum, 39/41 Sun Street, Waltham Abbey, Essex EN9 1EL. Telephone: Lea Valley (0992) 716882.

Preston Hall Museum, Preston Park, Yarm Road, Stockton-on-Tees, Cleveland. Telephone: Stockton-on-Tees (0642) 781184.

Tudor House Museum, Bugle Street, Southampton, Hampshire. Telephone: Southampton (0703) 24216.

Williamson Art Gallery and Museum, Slatey Road, Birkenhead, Merseyside. Telephone: 051-652 4177.

A museum of heraldic china is under construction at the National Motor Cycle Museum, adjoining the National Exhibition Centre, Birmingham. It will be the home of the National Heraldic China Collection. Further details are available from: 62 Murray Road, Horndean, Hampshire PO8 9JL.

DEALERS AND CLUBS

Most antique shops and flea market stalls are now eager to buy and sell crested china, as it is becoming so much better known and more desirable. One must be careful to refer to the *Price Guides* published on the subject, because often traders in their ignorance price items according to size, or perhaps in accordance with what they paid for them. There are, however, several reputable specialist dealers who can advise the collector.

The leading monthly mail order sales catalogue, which has been published for over ten years and offers Goss and all other makes of heraldic china, is available from:

Goss and Crested China Ltd, 62 Murray Road, Horndean, Hampshire PO8 9JL. Telephone: Horndean (0705) 597440. This company is the leading dealer and visitors are always welcome.

The following dealers do not publish a catalogue but keep extensive stocks:

Len's Crested China, Twyford Antiques Centre, Reading, Berkshire. Home address: 77 Gatewick Close, Slough, Berkshire, SL1 3SE.

Madoc Antiques (H.T. Aldridge), 48 Madoc Street, Llandudno, Gwynedd. Specialist in Welsh Goss.

Mrs D. M. Nicholas, Leintwardine, Craven Arms, Shropshire. Telephone: Leintwardine (054 73) 267. Specialist in Welsh border crests and models.

Swan Lane Antiques (Betty and Neville Malin), Swan Street, Warwick. Telephone: (0926) 400040. Commemoratives and fine English china. The biggest dealers in the Midlands for crested china.

Since the early 1970s the monthly catalogue of Goss and Crested China Ltd has been the major source of stock for collectors. Through the firm's open days many collectors have made friends and contacts. National fairs for crestologists are organised by two established clubs and are held alternately in the north and south of England. The Crested Circle is a friendly and informative club, publishing a magazine bi-monthly. The Goss Collectors Club was founded in the early 1970s and publishes a monthly magazine of news and views. Details of these two clubs may be obtained respectively from:

The Crested Circle: The Editor, Bob Southall, 42 Douglas Road, Tolworth, Surbiton, Surrey.

The Goss Collectors' Club: The Secretary, Mrs M. Latham, 3 Carr Hall Gardens, Barrowford, Nelson, Lancashire.